The Artistry Of Anthony Jackson

Andy Robertson

Published by
The Artistry of Anthony Jackson Copyright © 2020 Bassment Publishing

Layout and design
Pebbles and Welch Designs

Printed by
Caligraving Ltd

All rights reserved. No part of this publication may be reproduced, stored in a retrieval system or transmitted in any form or by any means – electronic, mechanical, photocopying, recording or otherwise – without the prior permission of the publishers. All correspondence concerning the content of this volume should be addressed to Bassment Publishing, 29 Holmden Avenue, Wigston, Leicester, LE18 2EG.

Bassment Publishing hereby exclude all liability to the extent permitted by law of any errors or omissions in this book and for any loss, damage or expense (whether direct or indirect) suffered by a third party relying on any information contained in this book.

A copy of the British Library Cataloguing in Publication Data is available from the British Library.

ISBN: 978-1-5272-7317-7

Contents

Acknowledgements — 5

Foreword — 6

Introduction — 7

Track	Title	Artist	
1	Clouds	Chaka Khan	9
2	Ruby Baby	Donald Fagen	19
3	For The Love Of Money	The O'Jays	25
4	Captain Caribe	Lee Ritenour	33
5	Grand Slam	Metro	39
6	Fly By Night	Lee Ritenour	47
7	Playboy	Teena Marie	53
8	Glamour Profession	Steely Dan	59
9	Tell Me a Bedtime Story	Quincy Jones	67
10	So Not To Worry	Chaka Khan	75

Acknowledgements

I would firstly like to thank my Mum and Dad for their constant support and belief in me in an ever-changing and challenging industry. Thank you for making sure I had the instruments to practise on and the lessons to go to, and for putting up with the endless hours of noise!

To my beautiful partner Sarah for her support and encouragement of this project and way beyond, especially at the times when I didn't believe there was an end in sight. Thank you for putting up with hours of absence working 'in the cave'.

To Melvin Lee Davis for his support, guidance, inspiration and, above all, friendship. Thank you for being instrumental in steering the project in the right direction and for adding your invaluable knowledge and experience.

To Nik and Mary at NPA management. Thank you so much for taking this on and believing in it when others were hesitant. For tackling every hurdle along the way with the utmost professionalism and making my dream a reality. I hope there will be more to come.

To Richard Pells at the Drum Academy in Leicester, UK. Thank you for the first class drum tuition and introduction to the wonderful world of music. I would not be making my living in music if it wasn't for you. It was you who first made me aware of Anthony Jackson through Dave Weckl's play-along material and I am eternally grateful.

To Gary Rackham, my first bass teacher and biggest inspiration to play the bass guitar. You were the reason I wanted to play bass in 1996 and subsequently wanted it to be my life. Thank you for your continued inspiration and being one of my closest friends for the last 25 years.

To Neil Hunter, thank you for your friendship and musicianship over the past 20 years, the countless album recommendations and education, and for taking care of every single electronic component I have turned up with for repair! Your keen eye and attention to detail added the finishing touches to this project.

Finally, to all the musicians I have worked with during my career, you have all helped to shape my musical understanding in some way, thank you all!

Foreword

Anthony Jackson! An inspiring yet intellectual giant in the world of the low sonic spectrum of the art of making music. I first came to know this amazing artist in the early 1970s through his bass work with R&B soul group The O'Jays. A co-writer of the legendary hit 'For The Love Of Money', one listen to that track and you knew you were listening to a master of the instrument. The precision of the groove; the use of a pick and the use of a phase-shifting effect etched his name in the history books among the innovative bassists of our time.

At that time there weren't many who would take the leap at being the focal point on bass, for a song that would over time be known and admired because of the bass groove. Anthony Jackson set a new standard for a generation of bassists to follow. His prowess would literally change the way we listen to music. His ability to draw you into his art while admiring the art he was contributing to was nothing short of brilliant. His ability to draw you into a groove with precision and occasionally stick a gem in the mix would have you picking up a bass yearning to learn. That is the essence of Anthony Jackson's mastery.

While touring Europe with Chaka Khan, I ran into Anthony when he was touring with Michel Camilo. We sat for a good chat... I shared with him how he literally changed my life in how I thought about playing the contrabass guitar, as I too played an extended range bass. I shared with him my desire to learn as much from his concepts as I could, because I was touring with an artist that he had recorded for.

Sure I could have put my own mark on the music he recorded, but my level of respect for his art kept me going back to playing his original grooves. I thought his contribution to the art of playing in a group setting, live or in the studio, added the most value to the work he was involved with. In a world that would come to produce synthesised bass (shout out to Greg Phillinganes) and the pop and pluck bass (shout out to Larry Graham), he refused to yield to that style of play. To those of us who understood the importance of playing fingered style bass, Anthony's style of play became more relevant to those of us who love his art.

Author Andy Robertson is a good friend of mine and also a fellow extended range bassist. We share a love and admiration for Anthony Jackson's art of playing. We often talked about how it would be great to have transcriptions of Anthony's work, both for bassists and also for other instrumentalists to research in order to get a good measure of his contribution to the arts.

Andy, an accomplished bassist and educator, shared with me that his inspiration for the book "was the discussions with me about the popularity/demand for a book dedicated to a very small percentage of AJ's work". This book of some of Anthony Jackson's work has been produced to give you an understanding of the essence of his thinking. The context of how music was being produced in the mind of the great Anthony Jackson. To listen is to emotionally engage... to see the work is to understand the journey taken through the creative process.

This book is necessary. This book matters. This book's time is right now! Andy has given the bass world a great gift... the musical world according to the legendary artistry of Anthony Jackson. I for one am proud to be associated with the subject and the author. Enjoy.

Melvin Lee Davis

Introduction

If you were to ask most of the highly respected bassists in the world today who they would cite as their greatest inspiration, many of them will give the same answer; Anthony Jackson.

I first became aware of Anthony Jackson while having drum lessons at the age of 14. An important part of my musical development in these lessons was playing along to backing tracks that featured the best in the business, and one of those was Anthony Jackson himself. At the time I had no idea about the musician I was listening to and the breadth and diversity of his work because I was only concerned with playing the drums! However, over the next few years my ear developed, I started to tune in to the musicians who appeared on these tracks, and before long I wanted to find out as much as I could about them and where else I could hear them play.

My hunger to learn was growing and in the late 1990s I began having bass lessons at music college. I was encouraged by my tutors to study some of the greatest players around, although at the time I shied away from Anthony Jackson's work because I just didn't have the musical understanding of what he was doing… the gap just seemed too great.

Over the years that followed I performed all over the world and met many fine musicians. So many of these players would perk up at the mention of Anthony Jackson, with universal appreciation across the board irrespective of style differences and musical preferences. Conversations with fellow bass players nearly always came back to the subject of AJ and his extensive discography alongside musicians of the highest calibre.

Eventually I decided it was time to push onwards and finally gain some kind of understanding of the Anthony Jackson mindset, and my study began. After much research and discussion of AJ's discography it seemed the real difficulty was knowing where to start! Some lengthy conversations with Melvin Lee Davis helped to pinpoint some of the more notable music where Anthony is featured, and after much deliberation the 'final 10' are presented in this book.

This book shows only a small fraction of Anthony's contribution to the world of music but features some of my favourite bass lines and also some of my favourite artists. I hope that the transcriptions, when seen together with the harmony which I have also included, will reveal some of the mysteries and illustrate some of the characteristics of Anthony Jackson's playing style and help you on your own voyage of discovery.

Track: **Clouds**
Artist: Chaka Khan
Album: *Naughty*
Composers: Nickolas Ashford, Valerie Simpson
Year Of Release: 1980
Bass Technique: Finger Style

'Clouds' is the opening track of this 1980 Chaka Khan album and a personal favourite. Anthony's work can be heard on another five tracks on the album, which features a stellar line-up of musicians. It seems to me that there is a particular magic between Anthony and drummer Steve Ferrone who also plays on this piece. The bass part was groundbreaking due to Anthony tuning his 4 string bass down a major third; all part of his quest to extend the range of the instrument, with his 6 string 'Contrabass' guitar becoming reality in the years that followed. The unison line at the start of the piece is particularly difficult to get under the fingers at first, but practising at a slower tempo and using all fingers in the fretting hand makes it definitely achievable! This piece features heavily what I call the '*AJ Stomp*'. His use of staccato quarter notes through the scales really adds movement to the track. This is a great introduction to Anthony's approach in the crafting of bass lines.

*There are two transcriptions for this piece, one in concert pitch for 5 string bass, and also a version for 4 string bass transposed to E minor and bass transposed down a major third.

Clouds

Clouds 3

Clouds 4

Track Fade --

Words & Music by Nickolas Ashford & Valerie Simpson. © Copyright 1988 Nick O Val Co. Inc. EMI Music Publishing Ltd. This Arrangement © Copyright 2020 Nick O Val Co. Inc. All Rights Reserved. International Copyright Secured. Used by Permission of Hal Leonard Europe Limited.

Clouds - Open C Tuning

(Tuning: E = C, A = F, D = B♭, G = E♭)

♩ = 115

Clouds – Open C Tuning 3

Clouds – Open C Tuning 4

Words & Music by Nickolas Ashford & Valerie Simpson. © Copyright 1988 Nick O Val Co. Inc. EMI Music Publishing Ltd. This Arrangement © Copyright 2020 Nick O Val Co. Inc. All Rights Reserved. International Copyright Secured. Used by Permission of Hal Leonard Europe Limited.

Track: **Ruby Baby**

Artist: Donald Fagen
Album: *The Nightfly*
Composers: Jerry Leiber, Mike Stoller
Year Of Release: 1982
Bass Technique: Plectrum

This cover of 'Ruby Baby' has more complex harmony than the original and is typical of Donald Fagen's work. AJ features on two tracks from the album, the other being 'I.G.Y.'. The swing feel is heavily established from the opening bar with the rests and short value notes playing a vital part in this unison line with the piano. Anthony's combination of staccato and smooth phrasing really gives the verse some shape, with the slides from A♭ - A in the fourth and eighth bars adding to the blues effect (this can also be heard more prominently at the piano solo).

It is convenient to play the bass line with the open A string in this first section although the piece transposes up to F# later on which will require the same pattern being fretted. Maintaining a smooth flow with the shuffle is key to this one!

Ruby Baby

Ruby Baby 3

Track: **For The Love Of Money**
Artist: The O'Jays
Album: *Ship Ahoy*
Composers: Kenneth Gamble, Leon Huff, Anthony Jackson
Year Of Release: 1974
Bass Technique: Plectrum

Anthony's iconic bass line on 'For The Love Of Money' quite rightly earned him a writing credit alongside band mates Kenneth Gamble and Leon Huff, with AJ laying this bass line down at just 21 years old! Producer Joe Tarsia added a Phaser and reverb effects to Anthony's part, creating the unmistakable sound of the intro – many artists have sampled the line since its initial release. The difficulty in playing this piece is in developing the stamina needed to play the 16ths with consistency as they're pretty much solid throughout. As such, it is important to note the placement of the rests, with a light touch in both hands aiding the stamina and effectiveness of the mutes. Undoubtedly the most well known of all the pieces in this book.

For The Love Of Money

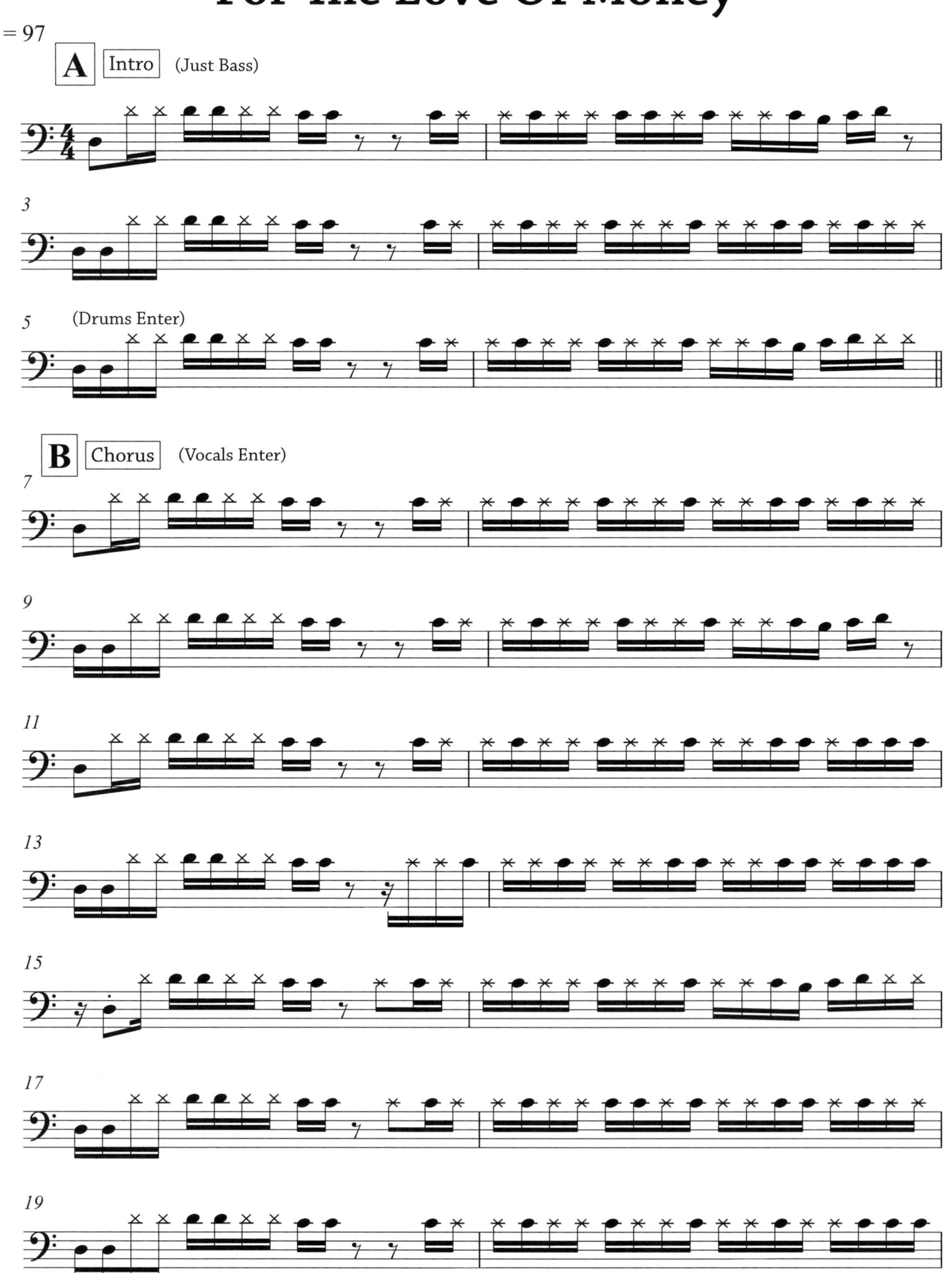

For The Love Of Money 2

For The Love Of Money 3

For The Love Of Money 4

For The Love Of Money 5

For The Love Of Money 6

Words & Music by Anthony Jackson, Leon Huff & Kenneth Gamble. © Copyright 1974 Mijac Music. Sony/ATV Music Publishing (UK) Ltd.
This Arrangement © Copyright 2020 Mijac Music. All Rights Reserved. International Copyright Secured. Used by Permission of Hal Leonard Europe Limited.

For The Love Of Money 7

Track: **Captain Caribe**
Artist: Lee Ritenour
Album: *Overtime* (Live CD/DVD)
Composer: Dave Grusin
Year Of Release: 2005
Bass Technique: Finger Style

The original version of 'Captain Caribe' was first released in 1976 by Earl Klugh and written by legendary film composer and arranger Dave Grusin. Anthony appeared on a number of Grusin's albums and live shows over the years, but it was this later version of 'Captain Caribe' that caught my attention. Once again Anthony is surrounded by an incredible line-up of fellow musicians on this live album, including Lee Ritenour, Dave Grusin, Ernie Watts, Harvey Mason, Patrice Rushen and Steve Forman.

The '*AJ Stomp*' is evident from the first bass entry and provides the track with forward movement. The bassline is actually quite straightforward, with the 'root-fifth' element appearing on several occasions, but the choice of note length and combinations of note lengths are hugely important in achieving the feel which AJ has. Learning to really listen to and lock in with the snare on the 2 & 4 will help to develop this feel, and a light touch with the fretting hand should help with the mutes.

Captain Caribe
(Live version from Lee Ritenour's *Overtime* DVD)

Captain Caribe 4

Track:	**Grand Slam**
Artist:	Metro
Album:	*Metro*
Composer:	Wolfgang Haffner
Year Of Release:	1994
Bass Technique:	Finger Style

Released in 1994 with an all-star line-up, 'Grand Slam' is one of the funkier takes from the album and really showcases Anthony's dexterity and accuracy while maintaining a solid theme in the bass part. The pushes, which are phrased with the bass drum, can be tricky to play consistently and accurately so beginning at a much slower tempo will really help to gain an understanding of the note placement. A light touch with the picking hand will be needed to achieve some of those 16th note runs, particularly when moving across the strings. Although some of the notes in the bass part might seem at first to conflict with the harmony, any change in chord tone is always met with strong support, all part of the genius that is AJ!

Grand Slam

Grand Slam 3

Words & Music by Wolfgang Haffner. © Copyright 1994 GEMA.

Grand Slam 5

Grand Slam 6

Grand Slam 7

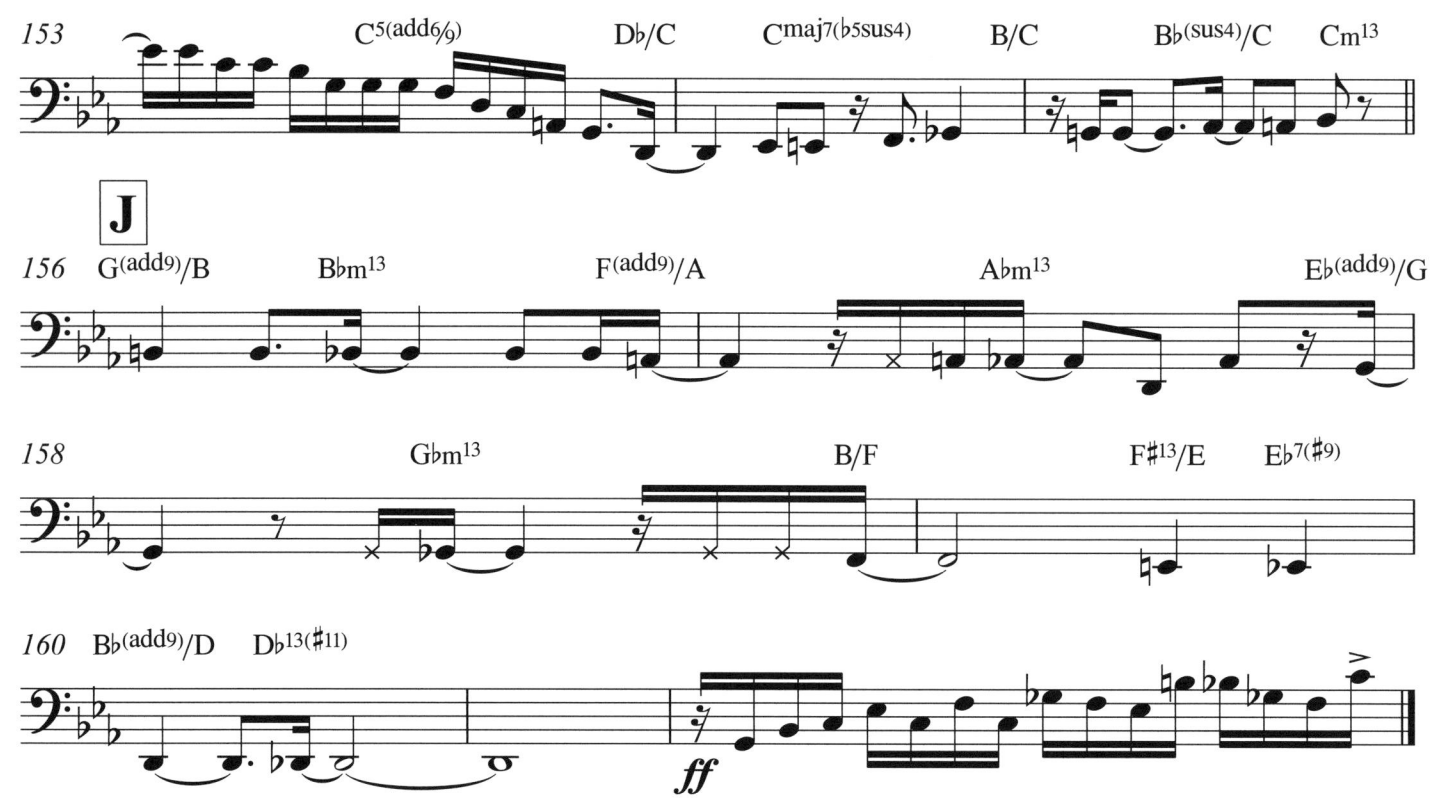

Words & Music by Wolfgang Haffner. © Copyright 1994 GEMA.

Track: ***Fly By Night***
Artist: Lee Ritenour
Album: *Captain Fingers*
Composer: Dave Grusin
Year Of Release: 1977
Bass Technique: Finger Style

Another one of Dave Grusin's compositions led by guitar virtuoso Lee Ritenour. Anthony appears on the first three tracks of the album with 'Fly By Night' appearing third. The classic '*AJ Stomp*' appears again here, which shows just how long this technique has been ingrained into AJ's style. The mutes play a big part in the bass line behind the lead guitar at the B Section and secure the 'head nodding and foot tapping' feel early on. Make sure to observe the staccato notes through the intro section, which will appear again later on in the piece. The outro section demonstrates AJ's ability to create an interesting line around a constant chord without being too busy, which is often difficult to achieve. Hopefully seeing AJ's bass line against the written harmony will help to unlock some of the mysteries and reveal the compositional ideas.

Fly By Night

Words & Music by Dave Grusin. © Copyright 1992 Sony/ATV Melody. Famous Music Corp. This Arrangement © Copyright 2020. Sony/ATV Melody.
All Rights Reserved. International Copyright Secured. Used by Permission of Hal Leonard Europe Limited.

Fly By Night 2

Fly By Night 3

Fly By Night 4

Fly By Night 5

Words & Music by Dave Grusin. © Copyright 1992 Sony/ATV Melody. Famous Music Corp. This Arrangement © Copyright 2020. Sony/ATV Melody.
All Rights Reserved. International Copyright Secured. Used by Permission of Hal Leonard Europe Limited.

Track:	***Playboy***
Artist:	Teena Marie
Album:	*Robbery*
Composer:	Teena Marie
Year Of Release:	1983
Bass Technique:	Plectrum

This 1983 release from Teena Marie features a stellar line-up of some of the best in the business. Anthony appears on three tracks on the album, and for 'Playboy' he is joined by 'pocket master' Steve Ferrone on drums. The close-working relationship and interplay of these two incredible musicians can be heard on many other albums, including some early Chaka Khan. Anthony's playing is wonderfully solid and consistent throughout this track with his attention to detail illustrated by his choice of note length. I believe this is one thing which sets Anthony Jackson apart from most other players – every note is a considered statement. Add this to his accuracy of unison lines and unmistakable fills, and another piece of master craftsmanship is formed. The ability to relax while playing the main line will help with stamina when playing this piece.

Playboy

Playboy 3

Words & Music by Teena Marie. © Copyright 1984 Midnight Magnet Music Publishing. EMI Songs Ltd. This Arrangement © Copyright 2020. Midnight Magnet Music Publishing. All Rights Reserved. International Copyright Secured. Used by Permission of Hal Leonard Europe Limited.

Playboy 4

Playboy 5

Track Fade -

Words & Music by Teena Marie. © Copyright 1984 Midnight Magnet Music Publishing. EMI Songs Ltd. This Arrangement © Copyright 2020. Midnight Magnet Music Publishing. All Rights Reserved. International Copyright Secured. Used by Permission of Hal Leonard Europe Limited.

Track:	**Glamour Profession**
Artist:	Steely Dan
Album:	*Gaucho*
Composers:	Donald Fagen, Walter Becker
Year Of Release:	1980
Bass Technique:	Finger Style

Released in 1980, 'Glamour Profession' is a particular favourite for Steely Dan fans. With an incredible list of musicians contributing to the album it's no surprise to find Anthony among them – he also appears on 'My Rival'. What is interesting in Anthony's line on 'Glamour Profession' is the use of rests at the beginning of the bars. It's natural (for me at least) to move with the harmonic rhythm rather than after it, but somehow nothing is lost in terms of energy and groove! The use of thirds and fifths under dominant 13th chords in the verses plays tricks with the ears at first, but the idea is straightforward and could readily be used when playing other pieces. The harmony is outlined so well in AJ's bass part that if the chords were taken out you would still hear them through the bass line alone.

Glamour Profession

Glamour Profession 2

Glamour Profession 3

Glamour Profession 5

Glamour Profession 6

Words & Music by Donald Fagen & Walter Becker. Registered Office: 130 Shaftesbury Avenue, London, United Kingdom, W1D 5EU. Registered in England. No. 10684804. © Copyright 1981 Zeon Music. Sony/ATV Music Publishing (UK) Ltd. This Arrangement © Copyright 2020 Zeon Music. All Rights Reserved. International Copyright Secured. Used by Permission of Hal Leonard Europe Limited. © 1981 Freejunket Music (ASCAP) admin. by Wixen Music UK Ltd. All Rights Reserved. Used by Permission.

Track: **Tell Me A Bedtime Story**
Artist: Quincy Jones
Album: *Sounds & Stuff Like That*
Composer: Herbie Hancock
Year Of Release: 1978
Bass Technique: Plectrum

This 1978 Quincy Jones release unsurprisingly features some of the finest musicians in the business. Anthony's distinct style is prominent on this track with some elegant work through the outro chord sequence. The rests in the opening bass pattern should be carefully observed as the daylight really adds movement to the track from the word go. As always, it's not just the choice of note which sets Anthony apart from other bass players; equally important are his decisions for note length and placement of rests.

String skipping is featured quite heavily in this piece with octaves, ninths and tenths appearing often. A light touch in the fretting hand will help to achieve the mutes, and with a track length just shy of seven minutes some stamina will be required!

Tell Me A Bedtime Story

Tell Me A Bedtime Story 2

Tell Me A Bedtime Story 3

Tell Me A Bedtime Story 4

Tell Me A Bedtime Story 5

Tell Me A Bedtime Story 6

Track:	**So Not To Worry**
Artist:	Chaka Khan
Album:	*Chaka Khan*
Composer:	Mark Gordon McMillen
Year Of Release:	1982
Bass Technique:	Finger Style

Both Chaka Khan and Anthony Jackson are favourites of mine and so to hear Anthony on a lot of the early Chaka albums is truly inspirational – it's also why the final track in the book is another Chaka Khan tune. AJ only appears on the one track on this particular album but certainly makes an impression as only he can. Once again, it is not just the choice of note but also the combination of note lengths that underpin this track with a serious pocket! The 16th note runs can be tricky but well worth some perseverance to help gain some understanding of AJ's approach around the chords. The effortless use of scales and arpeggios to highlight chord tones and the tasteful use of passing notes all help to define that this is most definitely Anthony Jackson in the chair. The outro section features some highly effective fills while still maintaining firm root note accents with the chord changes. A light touch in both hands will really help to achieve the tricky 16th note phrases.

There are two transcriptions for this piece, one in concert pitch for 5 string bass, and also a version for 4 string bass transposed to C minor with the bass transposed down a perfect fourth.

So Not To Worry

So Not To Worry 2

So Not To Worry 3

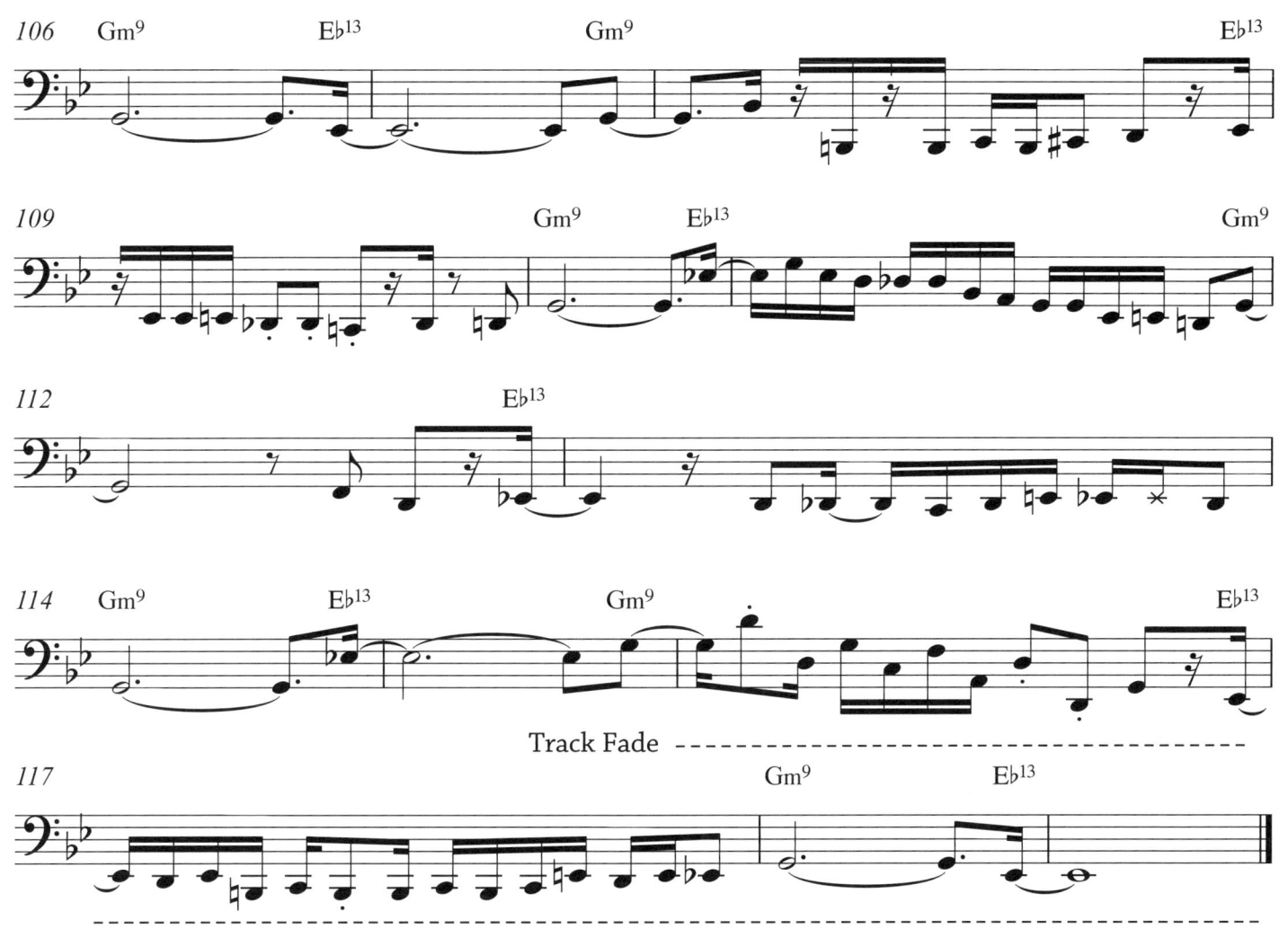

So Not To Worry - Open B Tuning

So Not To Worry – Open B Tuning 2

Words & Music by Mark McMillen. Registered Office: 130 Shaftesbury Avenue, London, United Kingdom, W1D 5EU. Registered in England. No. 10684804.
© Copyright 2019 Ikhan Sounds LLC. Spirit Music Publishing Ltd. This Arrangement © Copyright 2020 Ikhan Sounds LLC. All Rights Reserved. International Copyright Secured. Used by Permission of Hal Leonard Europe Limited.

So Not To Worry – Open B Tuning 3